Wood Carving for Curious Children:

The Easy-to-Follow Guide to Unlocking Children's Creativity with Quick & Fun Wood Handcrafts

By
Rodney Bock

© Copyright 2023 - All rights reserved.

The contents of this book may not be reproduced, duplicated, or transmitted without the direct written permission of the author or publisher.

Under no circumstances will the publisher or author be held liable for any damages, recovery, or financial loss due to the information contained in this book. Neither directly nor indirectly.

Legal Notice:

This book is protected by copyright. This book is for personal use only. You may not modify, distribute, sell, use, quote, or paraphrase any part or content of this book without the permission of the author or publisher.

Disclaimer Notice:

Please note that the information contained in this document is for educational and entertainment purposes only. Every effort has been made to present accurate, current, reliable, and complete information. No warranties of any kind are stated or implied. The reader acknowledges that the author is not offering legal, financial, medical, or professional advice. The contents of this book have been taken from various sources. Please consult a licensed professional before attempting any of the techniques described in this book.

By reading this document, the reader agrees that under no circumstances will the author be liable for any direct or indirect loss arising from the use of the information contained in this document, including but not limited to - errors, omissions, or inaccuracies.

Table of Contents

Introduction 6

    The Magic of Wood Carving 10

    Safety First: Carving with Confidence 14

Chapter 1: Getting Started with Wood Carving 20

    Tools of the Trade: Your Carving Companions 20

    Selecting Wood: Your Canvas for Creation 22

Chapter 2: The Art of Wood Carving 25

    Whittling Wonders: The Basics of Whittling for Kids 25

    Fundamental Carving Techniques for Young Carvers 32

Chapter 3: Bringing Your Ideas to Life 37

    Customizing Your Creations: Adding a Personal Touch 41

Chapter 4: Perfecting Your Craft 46

    Finishing Touches: Sanding, Painting, and Protecting Your Carvings 46

    Troubleshooting and Fixing Mistakes with a Smile 50

Chapter 5: Exploring Woodworking Adventures 54

    Beyond the Basics: Fun Challenges for Young Carvers 54

    Woodworking with Friends: Organizing Carving Workshops 57

Chapter 6: Reflecting and Showcasing 62

Displaying Your Carving Masterpieces... 62

Conclusion.. 70

Bonus: The Essential Tool Maintenance Guide.................................. 77

Video Tutorials... 85

Introduction

Imagine a young child sitting on a stool in the peace of the afternoon, his or her eyes concentrated on a block of wood, and small hands deftly holding a carving instrument. It's a scenario that evokes enduring images of imaginative discovery and a tender dance between creativity and skill. It's a time when the commonplace transforms into the remarkable and a lifeless piece of wood becomes the blank canvas of a budding artist's imagination. This, my reader, is the enchanted world of wood carving—a tradition that spans centuries and draws on children's natural inventiveness.

We're about to begin on a trip that has the power to capture your child's imagination, unleash their artistic potential, and deliver an engaging experience that goes far beyond the pages of this book as we explore the world of "Wood Carving for Children." This is a creative, self-discovery, and empowering journey into the heart of a time-honored skill. Welcome to a world where wood is more than just wood; it's a doorway to letting your child's magic out.

How to involve their kids in activities that are not only enjoyable for them, but also beneficial for their growth and development, is a challenge that many parents nowadays encounter. Although there is no denying the draw of screens and digital devices, we pay a tremendous price in terms of the chances we miss to engage in actual connection and hands-on creativity. This book addresses the difficult balancing act between technology and real-world experiences, which is a persistent struggle.

Through video games, cartoons, and social media, our kids are exposed to a constant stream of visual stimuli. Although they have their place in the modern world, these frequently leave our children without a genuine, tangible, and profoundly satisfying creative outlet. "Wood Carving for Children" is more than simply a book; it's the key to releasing your kid's creative and expressive potential.

But let's talk about the problems that parents and other caregivers face on a daily basis. Finding activities that truly engage kids or keeping them away from the alluring glow of screens is not an easy feat. This book recognizes your difficulties and offers a resolution. You'll see that wood carving provides kids an unlimited world of intrigue. It's an age-old craft that offers an antidote to the digital overload, an escape into the tactile world where the senses are engaged, and the mind is set free to wander, explore, and create.

Now, let's talk about the benefits of inviting wood carving into your child's life. Imagine your child developing patience as they carve intricate patterns, concentration as they focus on shaping the wood, and self-esteem as they complete their first wooden masterpiece. Consider the joy that comes with giving a homemade wooden gift to a loved one – the satisfaction of knowing they created something unique and meaningful. Think about the pride your child will feel as they learn to respect and work with natural materials, gaining an appreciation for the world around them. These are just a few of the invaluable benefits that this book aims to deliver.

But what exactly can you expect from the pages of "Wood Carving for Children"? This book is your comprehensive guide, a roadmap that takes you from the very basics to more advanced wood carving techniques, all in a format that is tailored for young readers. It's a journey that builds confidence step by step. Your child will learn how to choose the right tools, understand different types of wood, and embark on their very first wood carving project. They'll be guided through the process with clear, easy-to-follow instructions, vibrant illustrations, and creative ideas to inspire their imaginations.

Beyond the technical aspects, this book also nurtures the creative spirit within your child. It encourages them to explore their own artistic vision, teaching them to design and bring to life the wood creations that reside in their minds. Your child will discover the deep satisfaction that comes from watching their ideas materialize through their own hands. The process of carving wood becomes a conduit for self-expression, and every chisel, every stroke, becomes a stroke of empowerment.

Now, let's address the elephant in the room. You might be wondering, "Why should I trust this book? What makes the author an authority on wood carving for children?" These are fair questions, and it's important that you have confidence in the guidance we offer.

The author of this book brings to the table a wealth of experience and a passion for nurturing the artistic spirit in children. With a background in art education, the author has spent years working with young learners, understanding their unique needs, and crafting approaches that make learning an enjoyable and transformative experience. The author's expertise extends to the world of woodworking, where they have honed their skills through years of practice and a deep appreciation for the craft. More importantly, the author understands the hearts and minds of children, and they have tailored this book to ignite their imagination and guide them through a captivating journey of wood carving.

The beauty of this book is its approachability. It recognizes that not every child is destined to become a professional woodcarver, but every child can benefit from the joy of creating with their hands. This book is designed for beginners, for parents and caregivers with little to no prior experience in wood carving. It respects your need for clear and concise instructions and ensures that your child can start their wood carving adventure without any daunting hurdles.

But perhaps the most compelling reason to trust this book is the deep commitment to fostering creativity, imagination, and the joy of learning. It's a commitment that transcends the pages and embodies the author's belief in the transformative power of wood carving for children. As a parent or caregiver, you can be confident that this book is not just about teaching a craft; it's about enriching your child's life.

As you hold this book in your hands, you might be wondering if it's the right book for you, for your child. Let me assure you that if you seek to provide your child with a creative, hands-on experience that fosters imagination, patience, and self-esteem, then "Wood Carving for Children" is indeed the right book for you. If you desire a meaningful, screen-free activity that connects your child with the natural world, this book is your answer. If you long to see your child's eyes light up with pride and joy as they hold their wooden creations in their hands, then this book is your guide.

In the pages that follow, you will embark on a journey into the world of wood carving for children. You will witness the magic that happens when a child is handed a piece of wood and a carving tool. You will be a part of the transformation, the discovery, and the joy that comes with every chisel and every stroke. You will help your child unlock their creative potential, and in doing so, you will create memories that will last a lifetime.

This is not just a book; it's an invitation to a world where the ordinary becomes extraordinary, where the power of imagination meets the beauty of craftsmanship. It's an opportunity to nurture your child's creativity, to provide them with a gift that extends far beyond the tangible wooden creations they will make. This is the right book for you if you believe in the magic of a child's imagination and the wonder of their creative spirit.

So, let's take the first step on this enchanting journey. As you turn the page and delve into the world of "Wood Carving for Children," you'll be opening the door to a world of wonder, discovery, and transformation. Your child's adventure in wood carving awaits, and I promise you, it's a journey you'll both treasure forever.

The Magic of Wood Carving

The uncomplicated beauty of wood can be a revitalizing and enthralling experience for both kids and adults in a world where screens frequently take center stage. In all of its natural beauty, wood possesses a magic and a warmth that truly resonates with us. It's a painting that tells tales of the forest, of development and change, of vulnerability and strength. Wood carving is extremely magical due to the physical fascination of wood, its variety of textures, and the potential it provides as a creative medium.

We are about to begin on a trip together where we will explore the wonders of using wood as a creative medium. Consider holding a piece of wood in your hands and examining the grainy or smooth texture that reveals the wood's growth history. It's more than simply a piece of wood; it's a free invitation to delve inside, mold it, and uncover its hidden riches.

Your child will experience a primordial connection with something that precedes the digital age but is, in many ways, more relevant than ever as they interact with wood.

Children who carve wood are encouraged to use all of their senses to explore the environment, to pay attention to the details of the wood they choose, and to use the magic it contains. A sensory experience that is unrivaled in the digital world is created by the touch, smell, and even sound of the wood as it gives to the carving tool.

Think about the tale of a modest block of wood for a moment. It might be a remnant of a tree that has seen countless seasons or a piece of salvaged wood with a long history of its own. Every piece of wood has a special history and personality. Your youngster will see the knots, grains, and other inherent flaws that give the wood its unique appearance as they examine it more closely. These flaws, rather than taking away from the wood's beauty, add to its character and open up new creative possibilities. In the realm of wood carving, knots take the form of an animal's eyes, grains take the shape of a little forest, and flaws become the peculiarities of a quirky wooden creature.

Your youngster is invited to discover the natural beauty of wood as a creative medium and so become a part of its tale. The wood unveils its secrets during the carving process, allowing your youngster to create a story within its constraints. Children are able to create, tell their own stories, and enjoy the wonder of wood carving because of a strong bond they have with the material.

Imagine a little youngster picking up a carving tool and making their first hesitant cut on a block of wood for the first time. The transformation from the untouched block to the finished product, which now carries the distinctive mark of the child's imagination, is magical. The wood, which was once motionless and static, is changed into a living, breathing creation. This is the magic of transforming a piece of raw material into beauty, and it is the essence of wood carving.

Your child will enjoy the rush of discovering what is hidden in the wood as they carve. They will observe as the wood seemingly comes to life with each deft movement of the carving tool as their ideas take shape. The enchantment of wood carving lies in this process of change, where the ordinary is made extraordinary. It serves as a monument to both the power of imagination and the potential magic of a piece of wood.

What to Expect from This Book

After discussing the allure of wood as a creative medium, let's focus on what to anticipate from "Wood Carving for Children." This book is more than just a how-to guide; it's your key to realizing the transforming power of teaching your child to carve wood.

You can expect a thorough and user-friendly approach to wood carving, first and foremost. Whether you have prior woodworking expertise or not, this book is written with the beginner in mind. You and your child may start this trip with confidence since the directions are simple, the graphics are colorful, and there is step-by-step coaching.

We recognize that the safety of your child is of the utmost importance. You may discover comprehensive instructions on kid-friendly woodcarving techniques in this book. We offer advice on making a safe environment, employing safety equipment, and selecting the appropriate tools. We put the safety and enjoyment of your child's wood carving experience first since it is important to us.

The book is also a wealth of original thoughts. We are aware that every child is different and has a range of artistic interests. A wide variety of carving projects are available in "Wood Carving for Children," ranging from easy, enjoyable designs to more challenging ones that challenge your child's artistic abilities. This book contains something to spark your child's imagination, regardless of whether they are interested in the animal kingdom, fantastical worlds, or practical art.

Beyond wood carving's technical components, this book encourages self-expression and the spirit of creativity. By helping children to design and make the imaginary wood things come to life, it encourages your child to discover their own artistic vision. We think that the pleasure of wood carving extends beyond simply following directions and involves giving your child the freedom to express themselves creatively.

This book's journey through its pages is not only a solitary one. It's an invitation for you to spend quality time with your kids, connect with them over a common interest, and see how they develop. The art of wood carving promotes tenacity, patience, and concentration. It fosters a sense of self-esteem and pride that goes far beyond the finished product by giving your child a sense of success as they watch their ideas come to life.

You'll learn that wood carving is a flexible and dynamic skill as you read this book. It's a form of entertainment that can be enjoyed inside or outside, alone or with others. With your child, you can go on wood carving excursions in the comfort of your own home or take your works outside to connect with nature and draw inspiration from the surroundings.

In the chapters that follow, you'll delve into the practical facets of wood carving and discover the essential equipment, supplies, and methods. You'll look at projects ranging from the fanciful to the practical, and you'll see how your child develops as a wood carver as they become more assured and skilled with each piece they produce.

However, "Wood Carving for Children" is more than a simple instruction manual. It's an invitation to a world where your child may express their natural creativity, turn a piece of wood into a work of art, and discover the beauty of using their hands to mold their imagination.

You'll see the incredible metamorphosis that results when a child's imagination and wood carving come together as you proceed on this adventure. A sense of wonder, a connection to nature, and the joy of self-expression are all fostered by wood carving in addition to the creation of wooden figures. More than just carving talents, your child will learn life lessons that will help them in many facets of their future.

This book is an invitation to a world of creation, exploration, and transformation, so keep that in mind as we go further into the world of wood carving. It's a voyage that draws on the magical properties of wood, where the ordinary transforms into the exceptional, where your child's imagination knows no limitations, and where the artistic carving melds with the beauty of nature. The magic is waiting as we cut our way through the next chapters of this book, which serves as your entryway into the enchanted realm of kid-friendly wood carving.

Safety First: Carving with Confidence

There is an important issue we must address before starting our thrilling voyage into the realm of wood carving, and that issue is safety. As we introduce our children to the pleasures of wood carving, we must retain the notion that "safety first" is more than just a catchphrase. It is crucial to ensure a safe and secure setting since it will create the ideal conditions for a satisfying and joyful wood carving experience.

Like any hands-on endeavor, wood carving requires the use of precise tools, laser-like focus, and a certain amount of dexterity. In order to protect our children and instill in them a feeling of responsibility and respect for the tools they use, it is our duty as parents and caregivers to develop a set of fundamental safety principles.

1. **Supervision**: The presence of an adult or responsible caregiver is essential for younger children, especially those under the age of 10, when engaging in wood carving activities. When utilizing more sophisticated equipment or acquiring new skills, even older kids may need supervision.
2. **Tool Selection**: For your child's age and skill level, pick the appropriate tools. As their skills advance, progressively introduce sharper, more sophisticated tools after beginning with simpler ones with rounded edges.
3. **Workspace**: Make a dedicated workplace for wood carving that is spotless, well-lit, and uncluttered. Make sure the workspace is sturdy and that your youngster can comfortably reach the work surface.
4. **Safety Zones**: Create a "safety zone" surrounding the work area for your child to play in. This area should just contain the carving and be free of distractions and barriers.
5. **Proper Techniques**: Teach your child how to hold and operate carving tools properly. Stress the value of cautious, controlled movement to avoid accidents.
6. **Cutting Away from the Body**: Teach your youngster to always cut away from their body. This straightforward yet important rule aids in preventing unintentional self-harm.
7. **Sharp Tools**: Sharpen your carving tools. Accidents can result from using dull instruments since they need more effort and are more likely to slip.
8. **Use of a Carving Glove**: Encourage your child to wear a carving glove on the hand

that holds the wood when using sharp instruments, especially chisels. This glove offers supplementary defense against unintentional falls.

9. **Hands-on, Not Hand-in-the-way**: Remind your child to keep the hand that isn't carving behind the tool and away from the edge. This lessens the possibility of their hand being caught in the tool's path.
10. **No Rush**: Stress the value of perseverance and concentration. Rushing through a project increases the risk of thoughtless errors and mishaps.
11. **Clean-Up Routine**: Set up a cleaning regimen where your youngster is in charge of tidying up any wood shavings or other waste and putting tools back where they belong. A safe workstation is one that is organized.
12. **Emergency Plan**: Make sure your youngster is familiar with emergency procedures. This involves knowing how to administer basic first aid and how to contact an adult for assistance.

By following these crucial safety recommendations, you'll give your youngster a strong foundation on which to carve with assurance. When safety measures are implemented, wood carving can be a very safe and rewarding activity that gives your child the chance to hone both their creative talents and feeling of responsibility.

Proper Use of Tools

After establishing the significance of safety, let's examine how to use wood carving tools correctly. Understanding how to use these tools properly is essential to having a safe and happy experience since they are the key to unlocking the beauty of wood carving.

1. **Carving Knives**: Some of the most useful tools for cutting wood are carving

knives. They are great for intricate work and come in a variety of sizes and shapes. To lower the danger of mishaps, teach your youngster to use carving knives with a calm pulling action as opposed to pushing.

2. **Gouges**: Curved chisels, or gouges, occur in a variety of forms. They are used to shape the wood by forming hollows, curves, and shapes. To prevent chipping, teach your youngster to use gouges evenly pressured and in the direction of the wood's grain.

3. **Chisels**: Chisels are tools with flat blades used to create smooth surfaces and straight cuts. When using chisels, stress the value of maintaining the tool sharp and occasionally applying extra force with a mallet or hammer.

4. **V-Tools**: V-tools are perfect for making grooves and little details because they have a V-shaped blade. Ensure that the tool is precisely aligned with the desired cut when your child uses V-tools.

5. **Mallets and Hammers**: When using chisels and other tools, force is applied with the use of mallets and hammers. Teach your child to strike gently and precisely with the proper mallet or hammer for the tool they are using.

6. **Gloves**: The significance of a carving glove, particularly when using sharp tools, has already been addressed. In order to add an additional layer of protection, encourage your youngster to wear it on the hand that is holding the wood.

7. **Sharpening Stones**: It's essential to keep tools sharp for safe and effective wood carving. Teach your child how to use strops or sharpening stones to keep the tool's cutting edge sharp.

8. **Safety Grips**: Young carvers are further protected by the safety grips that some instruments have. These grips lessen the likelihood of injuries by making it more

difficult for hands to stray onto the blade.

By teaching your child how to use tools properly, you give them the abilities they need to carve with assurance and accuracy. Understanding how to use wood carving tools safely and successfully is the key to releasing the magic contained inside the wood. Wood carving tools are more than just tools; they are extensions of your child's creativity.

Safety Gear for Young Carvers

It's crucial to provide your child with the proper safety equipment in addition to teaching them how to use tools safely. Safety equipment not only protects, but also enables your youngster the self-assurance to experiment with wood carving without worrying about mishaps.

1. **Carving Glove**: The carving glove has previously been stated, but it is still important to emphasize. To prevent unintentional slippage, the hand holding the wood should be covered by a tight-fitting carving glove.
2. **Safety Glasses**: For eye protection, safety glasses or goggles are necessary. During carving, wood chips, dust, or splinters may fly, so make sure your youngster is wearing safety glasses to protect their eyes.
3. **Dust Mask or Respirator**: Fine dust produced during wood carving might be dangerous if inhaled. To safeguard their respiratory system, give your youngster a dust mask or respirator.
4. **Hearing Protection**: Certain carving tasks can be noisy, especially if mallets or hammers are used. You can protect your child's hearing by using ear protection, like earplugs or earmuffs.

5. **Apron or Smock**: Your child's clothing is kept clean and guarded against small tool-related scrapes and abrasions by an apron or smock. Choose one that is sturdy and simple to clean.
6. **Closed-Toe Shoes**: To safeguard their feet from falling tools or wood fragments, encourage your youngster to wear closed-toe shoes, ideally with a solid sole.
7. **Hair Ties**: If your child has long hair, make sure to pull it back so that it doesn't get in the way or get tangled in equipment.
8. **First Aid Kit**: Have a little first aid kit on hand. It has to contain adhesive bandages, antiseptic wipes, and any other special supplies your child might require owing to allergies or other health issues.
9. **Emergency Contact Information**: Make sure your kid knows how to contact an adult in case of an accident or injury and has access to emergency contact information.

By giving your child the proper safety equipment, you not only shield them from potential dangers but also impart to them the value of preparation and safety. Giving your child the appropriate safety equipment is an essential aspect of their wood carving journey since wood carving is a skill that encourages responsibility.

As you and your child begin this journey of wood carving, keep in mind that safety is not a limitation but rather a vital companion. You may set your child up for a successful and happy wood carving experience by following important safety precautions, comprehending tool use, and providing them with the necessary safety gear. We are now prepared to explore the creative possibilities that await us and go farther into the realm of wood carving with safety as our constant companion.

Chapter 1:
Getting Started with Wood Carving

A plain piece of wood can be turned into a priceless keepsake, a work of beauty, or a useful object using the time-honored craft of wood carving. This chapter will act as your guide on this thrilling adventure, whether you're a seasoned woodworker wishing to explore a new aspect of your craft or a total novice eager to enter into the world of carving. We'll examine the crucial components of beginning wood carving in this chapter, including the necessary equipment and how to choose the best wood for your projects.

Tools of the Trade: Your Carving Companions

Introduction to Basic Carving Tools

The fundamental tools that form the basis of this skill must be familiar to you before you start your wood carving adventure. Like with any art form, the secret to unleashing your creative potential is to master the tools. The fundamental carving implements that will become your closest friends are listed below:

1. **Carving Knife**: The spirit and lifeblood of wood carving is the carving knife. It is a multipurpose instrument with a pointed, sharp blade that is ideal for making fine details, delicate cuts, and complex designs. Look for a carving knife that fits your hand well and has a comfortable handle.
2. **Gouges**: Gouges exist in a variety of sizes and shapes, but they are always used to hollow down wood or make curves. For shaping and smoothing your carving, they are essential. Beginners ought to begin with a couple of basic gouges, such as

a straight and a V-gouge.

3. **Chisels**: Chisels are sturdy, straight-edged tools used to remove extra wood, tidy up edges, and make straight cuts. Similar to gouges, you should start with a basic set of chisels in various widths.

4. **Mallet**: To strike your chisels and gouges, use a weighted mallet. It enables you to use fine-grained force without endangering your hands or your tools.

5. **Sharpening Tools**: For precise work and clean cuts, keeping your carving tools sharp is crucial. To keep your tools sharp, spend money on honing stones, strops, or honing guides.

6. **Safety Gear**: Remember to practice safety. To safeguard your hands and eyes from potential harm, gloves, safety glasses, and a carving glove are necessary.

7. **Workbench and Clamps**: You'll need a sturdy workstation with clamps to keep your wood firmly in place if you want to carve effectively. This avoids slipping and guarantees your security.

Selecting Tools Suitable for Children

Getting the family involved in wood carving may be enjoyable, as can teaching kids how to do it. However, while working with young carvers, safety comes first. It's important to take into account a child's age, experience, and degree of supervision when choosing items that are appropriate for them. Here are several carvings implements suitable for children to get your kids started:

1. **Safety Carving Tools**: There are carving kits specifically made for kids that come with blunted or rounded blades. These implements lessen the possibility of mishaps while still letting kids enjoy carving.
2. **Supervision**: Children should always be closely watched during their carving sessions, regardless of the tools they use. Teach them the value of safe practices and appropriate technique.
3. **Gloves and Safety Gear**: Make sure your youngster is outfitted with the proper safety gear, such as gloves and goggles. Stress the significance of always wearing these items.
4. **Quality Wood**: Give them wood that is soft and simple to carve as a starting point. Pine, cedar, or basswood are all suitable options. The learning process is more fun in these woods because they are forgiving to beginners.

It's time to explore the world of wood choosing now that you've been familiar with the key carving tools and discovered how to make wood carving a fun activity for the whole family.

Selecting Wood: Your Canvas for Creation

Exploring Wood Types for Beginners

The choice of wood is an essential component in wood carving. Your project's outcome and your carving experience will be significantly influenced by the sort of wood you select. Starting with woods that are simple to carve and forgiving of errors is crucial for novices. The following wood kinds are appropriate for beginning woodworkers:

1. **Basswood**: The best wood for beginning carvers is basswood. It is delicate, fine-grained, and simple to handle. It is a popular choice for delicate details because of its light tone, which makes it possible to see your carving lines clearly.
2. **Cedar**: Cedar is renowned for its fine grain and lovely scent. It's another fantastic option for novices because it's gentle, light, and easy to carve. The rustic appeal of cedar gives your projects personality.
3. **Pine**: Because it is commonly available and reasonably priced, pine is a preferred material for novice carvers. It is soft, light in color, and has a fine texture that is great for practice because it is forgiving of mistakes.
4. **Butternut**: Due to its slightly softer texture than basswood, butternut wood is a fantastic choice for beginners. It is a joy to carve because of its creamy color and excellent texture.
5. **Redwood**: Redwood can be a little more fragile than other timbers, despite being lightweight and simple to carve. However, its organic red color gives your creations a distinctive touch.

Choosing the Right Wood for Your Project

The kind wood you should use depends on the specifications of your project, though for novices, basswood, cedar, pine, butternut, and redwood are acceptable options. Here are a few things to take into account while selecting the ideal wood for your project:

1. **Purpose**: What purpose does your carving serve? Are you constructing a sculpture, a piece of furniture, or something else? Different types of wood have

unique characteristics that make them better suited for particular uses.

2. **Size**: It matters how big your project is. Some types of wood are available in larger pieces, while others come in smaller bits. Make sure the wood you choose will fit the design's measurements.
3. **Design Complexity**: If your project calls for detailed details, pick a wood that will make it simple to carve the delicate features and fine lines. When creating intricate pieces, basswood is frequently the material of choice.
4. **Texture**: Take into account the texture you wish to create. While certain woods have a finer, more refined grain, others have a rougher, more rustic appearance. The final texture of your carving will depend on the type of wood you use.
5. **Budget**: Different types of wood have a range of prices. When choosing the wood for your carving, keep your budget in mind. Even while exotic hardwoods may be alluring, beginners would be advised to start with less expensive choices.

Choosing the perfect wood for your project and getting the necessary equipment are the first steps in the wood carving process. Understanding the fundamentals of tool choices and wood kinds is the cornerstone upon which your creative pursuits will bloom, whether you're creating complicated sculptures, useful objects, or simply introducing your kids to the world of woodworking. You're well on your way to mastering the craft of wood carving with your tools in hand and the ideal wood at your disposal. To help you hone your talents and release your inner artist, we'll delve deeper into carving techniques, projects, and advice in the next chapters. So, gather your carving implements and get ready to turn plain pieces of wood into original works of art.

Chapter 2:
The Art of Wood Carving

Few crafting techniques are as enduring and alluring as the art of wood carving. Wood carving is a craft that has captivated the hearts and minds of artisans and enthusiasts alike for generations, whether they are turning a plain block of wood into a true masterpiece or designing intricate motifs. We will explore the wonderful art of wood carving in this chapter, concentrating on whittling, one of its most simple and satisfying techniques. To provide a fun and secure experience for both children and adults, we'll go over the fundamentals of whittling, the techniques used, and the necessary safety precautions.

Whittling Wonders: The Basics of Whittling for Kids

Whittling is a delightful and rewarding technique that anyone can learn. It is frequently regarded as the starting point for more complex wood carving. It entails using a knife and a block of wood as the most basic tools for sculpting and carving wood. Whittling offers you a world of artistic possibilities and enables you to fashion small pieces of wood into a variety of shapes, including spoons and other tools as well as animals and figures.

The Magic of a Simple Knife

The fact that all you actually need for whittling is a nice pocket knife is one of its most alluring features. Whittling welcomes you with its simplicity, in contrast to many other arts that require pricey equipment. You can use a sharp knife as a magic wand to turn a piece of rough wood into a work of art.

For novices, a compact, folding pocket knife with a locking blade is ideal. You can operate securely and effectively since the blade locks into place to prevent unintentional closures during carving. Furthermore, keep your knife sharp and maintained because a dull blade might result in mishaps and dissatisfaction.

Choosing the Right Wood

A crucial component of whittling is choosing the proper sort of wood. For beginners, softwoods are typically the best option. For beginner projects, soft, simple-to-carve woods like pine, cedar, or basswood work well. When compared to working with harder types of wood, these woods are more forgiving and less likely to splinter.

You can look at other hardwoods like oak, walnut, and cherry when you're prepared for more difficult undertakings. These woods have a polished finish and are more durable, but they also call for greater skill and endurance.

Starting Your Whittling Journey

Whittling is more than just making something tangible; it's also about the experience, the perseverance, and the love of carving. In order to begin your whittling adventure, just do the following:

1. **Choose Your Design**: Choose a straightforward design or object to create to start. Start with something straightforward, such as a small animal or a geometric shape.
2. **Prepare Your Workspace**: Find a workspace with a sturdy table or workbench that is quiet and well-lit. Make sure it's clutter- and distraction-free. In order to collect wood shavings and dust, cover the table with an old cloth or newspaper.
3. **Secure the Wood**: To firmly secure your piece of wood, use a vice or clamp. As a result, there is less chance of an accident and it won't move while you're carving.
4. **Safety First**: Before you begin, it's essential to understand whittling safety measures, which we'll explore in more detail in the next subchapter.
5. **Start Whittling**: Start by taking out small, controlled pieces of wood slowly and carefully. To prevent accidents, always carve away from your hands and body. Always keep your fingers behind the blade.
6. **Patience and Practice**: Learning to whittle takes practice. If your initial attempts fall short of your expectations, don't give up. You'll develop your abilities and produce more complex carvings with practice.

Understanding Whittling Techniques

Let's get started with the techniques that will enable you to transform your wooden canvas into a work of art now that you've established the context for your whittling adventure. These methods will direct you in effectively shaping and carving your wood and are the fundamentals of whittling.

Basic Cutting Techniques

1. **Push Cut**: A fundamental cut is one in which you push the blade away from you. The majority of whittling techniques are based on this primary cutting motion.
2. **Pull Cut**: The pull cut entails pulling the knife in your direction. This method can be particularly helpful for shaping small details because it allows for the creation of fine, controlled cuts.
3. **Stop Cut**: A stop cut is a technique for drawing lines and defining boundaries. By pressing the blade into the wood, you create a small incision that serves as a template for subsequent cuts.
4. **Slicing**: Making long, shallow cuts across the surface of the wood is known as slicing. It's a great method for speedily removing bigger chunks of wood.

Shaping and Detailing Techniques

1. **Gouging**: Wood is scooped out during gouging in order to produce hollows or rounded shapes. It is frequently applied when sculpting a carving's concave regions.
2. **V-Cut**: The V-cut is made by combining two angled cuts into one point, which forms a V-shape. For example, this method can be used to add texture, make clothing folds, or highlight a bird's feathers.
3. **Relief Carving**: When carving a relief, the background wood is left untouched and a design that stands out from it is carved. This cutting-edge method is frequently employed in decorative carving.
4. **Smoothing**: Use gentle, controlled cuts to smooth your carving's surface after the rough shaping is finished to give it a polished appearance.

Grain and Texture

Whittling requires a thorough knowledge of the wood's grain and texture. The wood fibers' direction is referred to as the grain. To avoid splintering, carving must be done with the grain. Carving with the grain is typically simpler and produces cleaner cuts. To achieve a particular effect or texture, you might occasionally need to carve against the grain.

Also pay close attention to how the wood feels. Based on the growth rings and knots present, the same wood type can have different textures. Working with these variations can give your carvings more depth and personality.

Whittling Safety Measures

When carving wood in any way, especially whittling, safety should always come first. Even though whittling is a relatively risk-free activity, mishaps can still occur, so being ready and cautious is crucial.

Protective Gear

When whittling, always put on the appropriate safety equipment. This comprises:

- **Safety Gloves**: To prevent accidental slips or cuts on your hands, choose cut-resistant gloves.
- **Safety Glasses**: Avoid letting flying wood chips or splinters get into your eyes.

Carving Techniques

Technique is important for safety:

- **Carve Away from Your Body**: Maintain a constant distance from your body when carving, keeping your hands and fingers behind the blade.
- **Maintain a Stable Grip**: Hold the knife firmly in your hand, but don't squeeze it too much or you'll lose control. Support and stabilize the wood with your non-dominant hand.
- **Control the Blade**: Always maintain control over the knife. Avoid using too much force, which can cause falls and accidents.
- **Keep Blades Sharp**: Knives that are sharper than dull ones are safer. Slips are less likely when using a blade that is sharp.
- **Remove Distractions**: Carve in a calm, concentrated setting. Stay away from distractions that could lead to accidents.

Supervision for Kids

An important consideration is proper supervision when teaching children to whittle. Children should be assisted in the process and instructed on the value of safety. They must wear safety equipment while carving and can only use child-sized, age-appropriate tools.

First Aid Kit

Keep a small first aid kit on hand in case of cuts or other minor injuries. It's always preferable to be organized and have the tools you need on hand.

Respect the Tools

Always store your carving tools safely when not in use out of respect for them. Put them away from children's or animals' reach while keeping the blades safe.

Whittling Projects

Whittling unlocks a world of creativity, and there are countless project options. Here are some concepts to get you started on your whittling journey:

1. **Animal Figurines**: Make adorable creatures, such as birds, turtles, or rabbits. Start with straightforward carvings and work your way up to more intricate ones.
2. **Utensils**: Make useful items like letter openers, butter spreaders, and spoons. These initiatives combine form and purpose, making them both attractive and beneficial.
3. **Whimsical Characters**: Carve imaginative figures like gnomes, wizards, or fairies to let your imagination soar.
4. **Walking Sticks**: Create a decorative walking stick out of a plain stick by carving elaborate designs or animal figures onto the handle.
5. **Personalized Keychains**: Create personalized keychains for you or as thoughtful presents for loved ones. etch names, initials, or tiny patterns.
6. **Relief Carvings**: Create designs that stand out from the background, like flowers or intricate patterns, when you are more skilled, and try your hand at relief carving.

People of all ages can enjoy the deeply satisfying and adaptable craft of wood carving, and particularly the art of whittling. It provides an opportunity to express one's creativity, make a connection with nature, and practice patience and accuracy. Keep in mind that the journey and the satisfaction of making something lovely with your own hands are more important than the final destination.

Keep safety in mind at all times, hone your skills, and use your imagination as you begin your whittling journey. Your forays into wood carving might start with straightforward figures and implements, but with perseverance and practice, you'll soon be creating intricate patterns that will astound and motivate those around you. Grab a piece of wood and your reliable knife, then embark on a magical journey of creativity and craftsmanship with the help of the art of wood carving.

Fundamental Carving Techniques for Young Carvers

It's time to delve deeper into the fundamental carving techniques that will aid young carvers in producing stunning and accurate carvings now that we've covered the fundamentals of wood carving and the craft of whittling. Whatever your skill level, mastering these techniques will help you transform your woodworking projects into works of art.

Step-by-Step Instructions for Basic Carving Techniques

1. **The Push Cut**

The push cut serves as carving's cornerstone. It's the fundamental method for shaping and removing wood from your carving. How to execute a push cut is as follows:

1. Hold your carving tool firmly but not too tightly to begin. It should feel as though

the tool is an extension of your hand.
2. The cutting edge of your tool should be pointed away from you and at a slight angle to the wood.
3. Use your entire body to maintain control as you start pushing the tool into the wood. Moving your arm should be straight. Applying equal pressure is crucial.
4. When the tool is the desired depth, let up on the pressure and carefully lift it out of the wood.
5. To shape and remove wood as necessary, repeat the process.

2. The Pull Cut

A precise method frequently used to produce fine details is the pull cut. When working on your carving's more intricate components, it is especially helpful. A pull cut is done as follows:

1. As before, hold your carving tool so that the cutting edge is facing away from you.
2. Put the instrument where you want to make the cut in the wood and pull it in the direction of your body.
3. To direct and regulate the tool's movement, use your non-dominant hand.
4. Maintain a steady, controlled pull, adjusting the tool's angle as necessary to make the desired cut.
5. Once the desired detail or shape has been achieved, stop the pull cut.

3. The Stop Cut

The stop cut is an essential maneuver for drawing clear divisions between the various components of your carving. A stop cut can be made as shown here:

1. To define the area you want to separate, start with a push cut.
2. Once the initial cut has been made, angle the tool to draw a boundary line. A narrow groove in the wood should serve as the boundary line.
3. To direct further carving, follow the stop cut. By doing this, you can avoid accidentally removing wood from areas that you want to leave intact.

4. Scooping and Gouging

These methods are used to carve areas that are hollowed out or rounded. For adding depth and dimension, they are crucial. How to scoop and gouge is as follows:

1. To create the curve you want, hold your tool at an angle.
2. Apply gentle pressure while scooping out the wood to gradually deepen the curve or hollow.
3. For intricate details like eyes, feathers, or other rounded components, use gouging techniques.

5. V-Cuts

V-cuts are great for defining edges and adding texture. They entail cutting in two angled directions, meeting at a point to form a V-shape. How to create a V-cut is as follows:

1. To the wood, place your tool at an angle.
2. Make the first cut while slightly angling the tool in one direction.
3. Create a V-shape with the second cut by angling the tool in the opposite direction.
4. When adding details to your carving, such as feathers on a bird or folds in clothing, V-cuts are helpful.

Tips for Achieving Clean and Precise Cuts

1. **Use Sharp Tools**: Make sure your carving tools are always sharp. Sharp tools make cleaner cuts and are safer as well. To keep your tools' edges, regularly sharpen them.

2. **Work with the Grain**: Pay close attention to the wood's grain direction. Cutting smoothly is made easier when carving against the grain. Use caution if you need to carve against the grain to achieve a particular effect.

3. **Start with Soft Wood**: Start your carving journey with softwoods such as basswood or pine. Because they are forgiving and less difficult to carve, it is easier to make clean, accurate cuts.

4. **Plan Your Cuts**: Plan where and how you want a cut to go before making one. Consider the end result as you make your cuts, and be deliberate.

5. **Secure Your Workpiece**: To secure your piece of wood, use a clamp or vise. To carve precisely and safely, a workpiece must be stable.

6. **Practice Patience**: When carving, be patient. Rushing can result in errors and mishaps. Allow your carving tools to do their work patiently.

7. **Finger Placement**: Always keep your fingers behind the blade. It's essential for security and guarantees that you have command of the tool.

8. **Practice, Practice, Practice**: Wood carving is a skill that gets better with practice. You'll develop the muscle memory and control necessary for precise cuts as you carve more and more.

9. **Maintain Your Tools**: Maintain and clean your carving tools on a regular basis. To ensure their best performance, keep them free of debris and wood dust.

10. **Safety First**: Always adhere to safety regulations and put on safety gear, such as

gloves and glasses. In wood carving, safety comes first.

Young carvers can produce impressive and accurate wood carvings by mastering these basic carving techniques and using these advice. Keep in mind that developing a skill like wood carving takes time, so have patience with yourself and enjoy the process. Your carving abilities will develop with practice, enabling you to bring your imaginative visions to life in wood.

Chapter 3:
Bringing Your Ideas to Life

Have you ever experienced a sudden burst of creativity or had an idea that you just had to get out? That's where wood carving's true magic starts. We'll delve into the crux of the issue, "Bringing Your Ideas to Life," in this chapter. We'll talk about how creating a piece of art out of a basic block of wood can excite and satisfy you.

Simple and Engaging Wood Carving Projects

Beginning with simplicity, a vision is transformed into a real, carved work of art. We want to make certain that the young woodcarvers not only comprehend the fundamental methods but also experience a sense of satisfaction with each project they complete. We've chosen ten quick and interesting wood carving projects to get you started on the creative path because of this.

1. **Whittling a Wooden Spoon**: The small wooden spoon project is a great one for beginners. Learn to create a useful spoon by starting with a thin, flat piece of wood. You'll learn as you carve how even the smallest details can have a significant impact.

2. **Creating a Wooden Animal**: Create a small wooden replica of your preferred animal. Children can investigate a variety of shapes and textures in this project, from the smoothness of a fish's scales to the roughness of a lion's mane.

3. **Designing a Keychain**: Keychains are useful and simple to customize. Create a small wooden keychain with any design you like or your initials. There is room for both creativity and accuracy in this project.

4. **Making a Wooden Bead Necklace**: Make wooden beads for a necklace to combine carving and crafting. Create carved beads in various sizes and shapes, then string them together to make one-of-a-kind jewelry.

5. **Carving a Miniature House**: Carve a tiny house out of wood that has intricate doors and windows. This project helps kids develop their fine motor skills and teaches them to focus on even the smallest details.

6. **Crafting a Wooden Bookmark**: In addition to being useful, a wooden bookmark allows for imaginative design. Make a small motif, your name, or a favorite saying out of it.

7. **Whittling a Flower**: Make a delicate wooden flower by carving out its petals and leaves. With this project, you'll learn about 3D carving and incorporate a bit of nature into your works of art.

8. **Carving a Wooden Puzzle Piece**: Make a puzzle piece out of wood that is distinct in shape. These pieces can later be put together to create a custom wooden puzzle. Both problem-solving and creativity are on offer in this project.

9. **Whittling a Magic Wand**: Create your own magic wand to enter the world of fantasy. Make it enchanting by adding symbols, stars, and other finishing touches.

10. **Building a Simple Wooden Robot**: As you carve a tiny wooden robot, let your

imagination soar. It can be as imaginative or futuristic as you want.

The simple to slightly more difficult projects allow kids to gradually develop their confidence and skills. Keep in mind that the goal is to involve young carvers and motivate them to explore their concepts.

Building Confidence with Achievable Creations

The art of wood carving depends on perseverance and patience. The secret to success is taking small, doable steps, despite how intimidating it may initially seem. Let's look at how these projects not only let kids make lovely wooden objects but also help them develop self-confidence.

1. Confidence through Completing Projects

Each project's completion brings a sense of accomplishment. Children learn that they have the capacity to make something lovely with their own hands as they watch their ideas come to life. They feel better about themselves and are inspired to take on more challenging tasks in the future.

Imagine the satisfaction on a young child's face as they complete their first wooden keychain, animal, or spoon. Despite the simplicity of these projects, the sense of satisfaction is tremendous. As they proudly display their creations, their newly gained confidence will motivate them to take on the next challenge.

2. Building Skill and Dexterity

You will gradually improve your dexterity and wood carving abilities as you complete these projects. Whether it's how to precisely sculpt a tiny animal or how to make a useful item like a wooden spoon, every project teaches you something new.

You can practice using carving knives, chisels, and gouges by carving a wooden spoon, for instance. You'll discover safe and efficient ways to use each tool. Over time, your hands will become more coordinated, and you'll get a feel for the wood, knowing exactly how much pressure to use to get the desired effect.

3. Embracing Creativity

In addition to imitating existing objects, wood carving encourages you to explore your own creativity. There are many opportunities for customization with these projects. Children can experiment with designs, add their own special touches, and exercise their creativity. The development of their artistic confidence depends on this freedom of expression.

Kids can pick the pose, the expression, and even the kind of wood they want to use when carving an animal out of wood, for instance. Through their carvings, they are able to express their personalities and creativity.

4. Learning Patience and Persistence

The art of wood carving requires patience. It teaches kids the importance of taking their time to get the job done right. They will develop an appreciation for both the process and the end result as they complete these projects. Even though mistakes may occur, they can also serve as opportunities for growth.

Try to picture a youngster carving a wooden puzzle piece. To get the shape just right, it might take a few tries, but with perseverance and patience, they'll see it through to the end. The ability to persist is a crucial life skill that goes beyond wood carving.

5. Encouraging Problem-Solving

Even the simplest wood carving projects frequently require problem-solving. These projects offer chances to confront problems and come up with inventive answers, whether it's figuring out how to build a sturdy base for a wooden house or figuring out how to attach a keyring to a wooden keychain.

For instance, kids may need to consider how to attach movable limbs or make sure that it stands upright when carving a wooden robot. Critical thinking and resourcefulness are fostered through this method of problem-solving.

These ten easy wood carving activities for kids go beyond simple artistic endeavors. They are chances to increase self-assurance, acquire knowledge, value creativity, practice patience, and promote problem-solving. Young carvers will develop a love for the craft of wood carving as they work through these projects, which will last them a lifetime. They will also be able to bring their ideas to life. So grab some carving implements, some wood, and let your creative juices flow.

Customizing Your Creations: Adding a Personal Touch

Ten easy and interesting wood carving projects were used to explore the joy of bringing your ideas to life. Let's go one step further and explore the craft of customizing your works. Your carved pieces will become more distinctive and will promote creativity and individuality if you give them a personal touch. We'll look at how to add your own style and personality to your carvings in this chapter.

Encouraging Creativity and Individuality

The fact that wood carving is more than just exact replication of patterns and designs is one of its most appealing features. It provides a platform for self-expression and a chance to highlight your uniqueness. You're not just following a set of instructions when you customize your products; you're also letting your creativity run wild. Here are some tips for fostering originality and creativity in your wood carving projects:

1. Choose Your Designs

While the starter projects we've provided are great for learning the fundamentals, as your skill with wood carving develops, you'll be able to start picking your own designs. Here is where creativity really takes off. You can carve a design that symbolizes a special memory or an object that has personal significance to you, such as a favorite animal or symbol.

You might carve a butterfly because it makes you think of a lovely day in the park, or you might carve a star because it represents your dreams. It will be more enjoyable to carve if you select patterns that speak to you.

2. Experiment with Colors

Wood carving isn't just limited to the color of the raw material. By experimenting with colors, you can add your own flair. You can make your creations more colorful and unique by using acrylic paints or wood stains.

For instance, if you're carving an animal out of wood, you could paint it to look like your preferred real-life animal. Alternately, paint your favorite colors on the wooden puzzle piece you carve. When it comes to color customization, the options are virtually limitless.

3. Incorporate Text and Personal Messages

You can add text or individualized messages to your carvings to make them extra-special. It might be a dedication, a name, a date, a quick quote, etc. These messages can transform a straightforward wooden object into a priceless present for a friend or relative.

Imagine engraving a significant quote on a wooden bookmark for a friend. They will remember your kindness each time they open their book.

4. Mix and Match Styles

When carving wood, don't be afraid to mix up different styles. For instance, you can add a modern twist while combining traditional design elements. This blending of styles can produce unique and captivating works.

You can combine a traditional spoon shape with a modern handle design when carving a wooden spoon. You are free to explore and try out various styles since it is your creation.

5. Add Texture and Details

Since wood carving is all about the details, giving your creations distinctive textures and details can help them stand out. You can sculpt complex designs, scales, fur, or any other texture that goes well with your concept. These particulars not only enhance the aesthetic appeal of your carvings but also draw attention to your skill.

Consider including details like shingles on the roof or bricks on the walls when carving a wooden house, for instance. These minor adjustments can advance your project.

Techniques for Customizing Designs

After examining how personalizing your works can foster originality and creativity, let's examine some methods that will enable you to give your wood carving projects a unique touch:

1. Relief Carving

Carving a design that stands out from the background is known as relief carving. With this method, you can produce lovely three-dimensional effects. For example, you could carve a flower that protrudes from the surface of the wood to give it depth and dimension.

2. Chip Carving

In the art of chip carving, tiny pieces of wood are removed to produce intricate patterns and designs. It's an excellent way to give your carvings texture and details. Try chip carving to add delicate motifs or geometric designs to your projects.

3. Inlay

Cutting a design into the wood and then filling it with another substance, like contrasting wood or even colored epoxy resin, is known as inlay. You can use inlay to add beautiful and distinctive designs, such as small images or initials, to the center of your carvings.

4. Pyrography

Pyrography, also known as wood burning, is a method for imprinting designs on the surface of wood using a heated tool. You can now add exact and elaborate patterns, symbols, or text. It's a flexible technique for personalizing your works.

5. Stains and Finishes

Try out various wood finishes and stains to alter the appearance of your carvings. While coatings like varnish or wax can give your creations a polished and professional look, stains can add color and depth.

You can create one-of-a-kind and personalized wood carving projects that showcase your sense of style, personality, and creativity by fusing these techniques and experimenting with them. Customizing your creations can turn them into poignant and lovely works of art, whether you're carving them as a gift for a loved one or just for your own enjoyment.

So don't be afraid to add a personal touch to your wood carvings. Allow your imagination to run wild and observe how your carvings transform from simple wood pieces into unique and imaginative expressions of you.

Chapter 4:
Perfecting Your Craft

Finishing Touches: Sanding, Painting, and Protecting Your Carvings

Greetings, young woodcarvers! We will examine the craft of perfecting your wood carving projects in this chapter. You've already set out on an interesting journey, discovered the fundamentals, and produced some incredible works. It's time to advance your abilities at this point.

This chapter will be dedicated to providing the "finishing touches" that can elevate a good carving to greatness. We'll talk about the fine art of getting a smooth finish, look at painting methods to give your artwork life, and discover how to safeguard your labor of love so it lasts for generations.

Finishing Touches: Sanding, Painting, and Protecting Your Carvings

Let's first grasp why honing your craft is so crucial before getting into the specifics. Wood carving can be compared to storytelling. Your carving is like a book, and the cover and illustrations are the finishing touches. A carving that has been expertly finished not only looks better, but also effectively conveys your ideas. Consequently, let's start with the first chapter:

Achieving a Smooth Finish

Your woodwork may have some rough spots even after careful carving, as you may have noticed. It all comes down to transforming those jagged edges into something velvety and polished to achieve a smooth finish.

1. Sandpaper Selection: The secret technique that transforms your carvings from rough to refined is sanding. You'll need sandpaper in various grits to get started. When removing material quickly, coarser grits like 60–100 are used; for smoothing, finer grits like 22–400 are used. Work your way up to the finer grits starting with the coarser ones.

2. Sanding Techniques: Moving with the grain is essential for effective sanding. This implies that you'll go with the grain of the wood rather than against it. This gives you a smoother surface and stops the wood from splintering. Start with light, even strokes, then move on to finer grits as the wood smooths out.

3. Tackling End Grain: The wood fibers are most exposed along the end grain, making it challenging to sand smoothly. Be extra gentle when concentrating on these areas because they may be more prone to splintering.

4. Inspecting Progress: As you sand, don't forget to check your work frequently. Sometimes, a particular area may require more focus. If you come across any difficult areas, take extra care with them and continue working until they are smooth.

5. Wet Sanding: If you want an exceptionally smooth finish, you can also try wet sanding.

This involves using water to lubricate the sandpaper, which can help you achieve a glass-like surface.

Painting Techniques for Wood Crafts

Let's now give your creation some color! Your wood carving may benefit from painting to highlight the details and add a personal touch. Keep in mind that there are no strict guidelines for painting wood carvings. Your creativity and vision are everything. Here are some strategies to take into account:

1. Choosing the Right Paint: Wood can be painted with oil, acrylic, or watercolors. Your comfort level and desired outcome will influence your decision. Acrylic and oil paints produce vibrant, opaque colors, while watercolor offers a transparent, delicate appearance.

2. Base Coating: Initially, apply a basecoat. It could be a combination of colors or just one. The remainder of your painting will take on this tone after this. Before continuing, don't forget to give it time to completely dry.

3. Layering and Blending: Here is where your originality really shines. Paint in layers to create depth and dimension. You can use bold strokes for a more distinct appearance or color blending for a soft transition. Try out various brushes, sponges, and even your fingers to see which one suits your project the best.

4. Dry Brushing: With this method, a nearly dry brush and little paint are used. It works wonders for highlighting your carving's highlights and bringing out its finer details.

5. Staining: Utilizing wood stains is an additional choice. These add color while enhancing the wood's natural grain. You can choose a stain's shade to match your design because they come in a variety of tones.

6. Sealing and Protecting: It's crucial to seal your painting once you're satisfied with it to keep it from deteriorating. For this, you can use clear finishes or varnishes. These give your carving a lovely sheen in addition to protecting your paint.

Applying Protective Finishes

It's critical to safeguard your labor of love now that your carving is smooth and exquisitely painted. Applying protective finishes is crucial to ensuring that your masterpiece endures the test of time because wood can be sensitive to environmental factors like moisture and sunlight.

1. Varnish: One of the most popular protective finishes is varnish. Your carving is protected from water and UV deterioration by a strong, transparent layer that is created as a result. Varnishes come in a variety of finishes with varying sheen levels, including matte, satin, and gloss.

2. Oil Finish: Popular oils for wood carvings include tung, linseed, and Danish. They get deep inside the wood, feeding it and bringing out its natural beauty. A warm, rich finish that is appealing to the touch and eye is the end result.

3. Wax Finish: Beeswax and carnauba wax are examples of wax finishes that provide a more subdued level of protection. They impart a soft, warm sheen to your carving and are frequently chosen for their pleasant scent. Applying and reapplying wax is simple.

4. Shellac: Another protective coating made from natural materials is shellac. It dries quickly and offers a superior barrier of protection. To achieve particular effects, it can be used alone or in conjunction with other finishes.

5. Lacquer: For ornamental and practical carvings, lacquer creates a hard, glossy finish. For a high-gloss shine, it can be built up in layers and dries quickly.

Do not forget to apply protective finishes according to the manufacturer's instructions. For best results, careful planning and execution are essential. Once your carving has been properly preserved, you can proudly display it because you know its color will not fade over time.

It takes time and effort to hone your craft, but the journey is rewarding. Your carvings will retain the artistry and work you put into each one by being sanded, painted, and protected in addition to improving their appearance. Your wood carvings will genuinely transform into works of art as you advance in your ability to apply these finishing touches. So keep honing your skills and practicing; before long, you'll be producing works of art that will endure for future generations.

Troubleshooting and Fixing Mistakes with a Smile

Before we begin this lesson, I want to share a little secret with you. No matter their level of experience, everyone who carves wood makes mistakes. It's okay because it's a necessary component of the journey. This chapter will cover common issues that might arise while you are carving wood, as well as how to resolve them amicably.

Common Issues and How to Address Them

1. **Chips and Tear-Out:** Chipping or tear-out is one of the most typical problems with wood carving. When the wood fibers break or are pulled out, a jagged surface results. The answer? hone your implements! More tear-out may result from dull tools. Additionally, cut against the grain rather than with it. To avoid putting unnecessary pressure on your tools, move slowly and keep a firm grip.

2. **Uneven Surfaces:** Your carving's surface might occasionally not be as even or smooth as you'd like. If you want to fix this, think about resharpening your tools and pay attention to how you're holding them. To create a uniform surface, make small, precise cuts.

3. **Over-Cut or Under-Cut:** When you cut more wood than you intended, it's called over-cutting; when you cut too little, it's called under-cutting. Be at ease; both problems are resolvable. Overcuts can be creatively incorporated into your design by adjusting your plan or gluing a piece of wood back in place. Use filler to cover undercuts or carefully remove adjacent wood to the desired depth.

4. **Splintering:** Wood fibers can splinter or fracture, leaving behind jagged edges. Avoid carving against the grain, use sharp tools, and use a lighter touch to address this. If splintering does occur, you can sand the area for a smooth finish and glue the splinters back into place.

5. **Design Flaws:** A design might occasionally not work out as planned. Be not disheartened. Use it as a chance to be imaginative. Change your design as you go, include something extra, or create something entirely new. Unexpected design changes have given birth to many masterpieces.

Turning Mistakes into Learning Opportunities

The real secret is that every error provides a chance for a woodcarver to improve. Even though they can be upsetting, mistakes are an essential part of your journey. Let's look at some ways to make those frowns into smiles:

1. Stay Positive: It's simple to become irate when an error occurs. However, make an effort to view it as a chance to grow and learn. Be optimistic at all times. Keep in mind that even seasoned woodcarvers make mistakes; this is how they develop their skills.

2. Analyze and Reflect: Analyze what went wrong for a moment. Was the problem with the tool, the technique, or the design? Finding the underlying cause can help you steer clear of repeating the error in the future.

3. Seek Guidance: Never hesitate to seek out assistance or counsel. Join a club or online community for woodcarvers where seasoned artists can provide advice and guidance. A great way to develop your skills is to learn from other people's experiences.

4. Practice Patience: Like any form of art, carving in wood demands patience. Keep your projects on schedule. Take your time, particularly after a setback. Sometimes taking a break and returning with new eyes can make all the difference.

5. Embrace Creativity: Keep in mind that errors can inspire brand-new, unanticipated creative possibilities. Be willing to modify your project to include the error or even turn it into a distinguishing feature.

6. Keep a Woodcarving Journal: Think about keeping a woodcarving journal where you record your projects, the errors you make, and how you fix them. This journal can be a useful resource and a reminder of your accomplishments.

Remember that every artist has to overcome challenges as they make their way through the woodcarving process. Everything is a step in the process. A beginner and a master are differentiated by how they respond to these difficulties. So, don't let mistakes demotivate you. Accept them as stepping stones on your journey to mastering the art of woodcarving.

Chapter 5:
Exploring Woodworking Adventures

Beyond the Basics: Fun Challenges for Young Carvers

The world of woodworking offers countless opportunities. It's important to keep in mind that you don't have to complete these challenges perfectly the first time. It's about the excitement of discovery, the thrill of innovating, and the priceless lessons you'll pick up along the way. Let's start with some imaginative woodworking projects to advance your skill set:

Creative Woodworking Tasks for Skill Development

1. **Whittling a Wooden Spoon:** A traditional woodworking project that teaches you about round carving is whetling a wooden spoon. It's an enjoyable and useful challenge. Both the handle and the bowl need to be shaped carefully. You will learn about grain direction as you complete this project, which is crucial for the strength and stability of your creations.
2. **Relief Carving a Leaf:** On a flat surface, a three-dimensional design is carved in relief. Try your hand at carving a straightforward leaf with fine details and veins. Your ability to work with different depths will improve as a result of this project, enabling you to give your carvings texture and visual interest.
3. **Joinery Practice:** The skill of joining wood pieces together to form structures is known as joinery. Work on simple joints like the butt joint, dovetail joint, or mortise and tenon joint to test your skills. By using these joints to construct small wooden boxes or frames, you can improve your woodworking abilities while also

producing useful items.

4. **Wood Burning:** Pyrography, another name for wood burning, is a distinct form of art. Use a wood-burning pen to add designs or patterns to your wooden creations. Your woodworking projects will take on a whole new dimension thanks to this technique, which also lets you play around with shading and minute details.

5. **Turning on a Lathe:** Using a lathe to turn wood is a thrilling woodworking experience. You can make cylindrical shapes like candlesticks, pens, and even tiny bowls using a lathe. Precision and knowledge of how wood behaves in rotation are essential for turning.

6. **Inlay and Marquetry:** By putting pieces of one wood on top of another, inlay can produce beautiful patterns and designs. Marquetry is the art of inlaying various types of wood or veneer to produce intricate pictures. These two methods offer countless opportunities for creativity.

Building on Your Carving Expertise

Now that you've completed these imaginative woodworking projects, it's time to advance the carving skills you've acquired so far. You have the potential to make extraordinary pieces as a young carver. Here are a few difficult woodworking challenges that will test you and advance your abilities:

1. **Carving a Miniature Figure:** Whether carving characters or animals, accuracy and close attention to detail are essential. Whether you choose to draw a tiny animal or a beloved fictional character, this exercise will help you hone your fine motor skills and capture the essence of your subject.

2. **Wood Sculpture:** Try your hand at some wood sculpture. Create a piece of art that

goes beyond useful woodworking by picking a theme or an abstract idea. Depending on how you see them, wood sculptures can be expressive, abstract, or realistic. You're free to unleash your creativity during this adventure.

3. **Furniture Making:** Making your own furniture is a satisfying activity. Start with a modest undertaking, like building a side table or a bookshelf. You will learn about structural integrity, measurements, and the value of finishing for durable pieces from this adventure.

4. **Wooden Instruments:** Ever wanted to design your own musical instrument? Making wooden musical instruments is a unique challenge that combines woodworking and music, whether it's a straightforward percussion instrument like a drum or a more intricate one like a guitar. It presents an opportunity to investigate the relationship between art and purpose.

5. **Carving with Exotic Woods:** Consider working with exotic woods if you want a real challenge. These woods frequently have more intricate grain patterns, are harder, and come in a variety of gorgeous hues. They can, however, be less forgiving, making accuracy and attention to detail crucial.

6. **Woodworking Joints Mastery:** Explore the world of woodworking joints in detail. Investigate intricate joinery methods, such as the sliding dovetail or bridle joint. By mastering these complex joints, you can make intricate, sturdy, and gorgeous woodwork.

7. **Collaborative Woodworking:** Join forces on a joint project with other young carvers or family members. It might be a substantial sculpture, a piece of furniture, or whatever else you can imagine. Together, you can make something truly unique while improving your communication and teamwork skills through collaborative

woodworking.

Do not forget that it is acceptable to make mistakes as you embark on these woodworking adventures. Making mistakes, in fact, is an essential component of learning. Every error serves as a disguised lesson that directs you toward innovation and improvement. Challenges shouldn't deter you; instead, welcome them with a smile and the knowledge that you're developing as a woodworker and a woodcarver.

Woodworking with Friends: Organizing Carving Workshops

Collaborative Learning and Skill Sharing

The chance to collaborate with friends and other enthusiasts is one of the most amazing aspects of woodworking. Workshops for woodworking are the ideal setting for group learning and skill-sharing. The opportunities are endless when you collaborate with friends. You can take on challenging tasks, investigate various carving techniques, and draw inspiration from one another.

Imagine yourself and your friends assembling around a sturdy workbench, each carrying a piece of wood and a set of carving tools. Watching everyone's creativity come to life as they turn a simple block of wood into a lovely piece of art is inspiring. Along with making the experience more enjoyable, traveling on this creative journey with friends will hasten your development as a woodworker.

Here are a few ways to make woodworking with friends an adventure of its own:

1. **Choose a Theme:** For your group project, choose a theme. Animals, mythical

creatures, or even abstract patterns could be used. Your woodworking adventure will become more engaging and challenging by having a theme.

2. **Tool Exchange:** Request that everyone bring their carving supplies. In this manner, you can experiment with various tools and pick up new skills from one another.

3. **Group Critique:** Have a group discussion about your projects after you've finished them. Discuss your opinions and suggestions for each other's work. Everyone benefits from constructive criticism to become more skilled.

4. **Friendly Competition:** Organize a competition for amateur woodworkers. Whoever can produce the most impressive piece in the allotted time wins. The excitement of competition can inspire motivation and creativity.

5. **Document the Journey:** Document your group's woodworking adventure with photos or a video. Not only is the outcome important, but also the memories you make with your coworkers.

Hosting Your Own Wood Carving Workshop

You might feel compelled to impart your knowledge to others as your woodworking skills and confidence grow. Organizing your own wood carving workshop can be a really rewarding experience. It's an opportunity to share knowledge, pick up new skills, and build a community of like-minded wood enthusiasts.

The following steps will help you launch your own wood carving workshop:

1. Set Your Goals:

Define the goal of your workshop before you start. Do you want to explore more complex techniques, work on a specific project, or instruct beginners in the fundamentals of wood carving? You can effectively structure your workshop by establishing clear goals.

2. Gather Materials:

Make sure your workshop is equipped with all the supplies and tools it needs. Think about the kind of wood you'll use, the carving implements you'll need, and any safety gear like gloves and goggles. Create a checklist to make sure everything is in place.

3. Create a Lesson Plan:

Describe the structure and content of your workshop. Hands-on demonstrations are followed by an introduction to wood carving. Think about the sequence in which you'll teach the various techniques, and make sure to allow time for practice.

4. Promote Your Workshop:

Inform people about your workshop. To draw participants, you can make use of social media, neighborhood message boards, or word-of-mouth. Be specific about the workshop's date, time, location, and any associated costs.

5. Safety First:

Start off your workshop by focusing on safety. Provide safety instructions throughout the session and demonstrate safe tool handling to your participants. Keep a first aid kit close by at all times, just in case.

6. Hands-On Experience:

Start by letting participants get their hands dirty. Allow them to feel the wood, play around with carving implements, and design their first straightforward project. Encourage inquiries and provide direction as they work.

7. Foster Creativity:

It's crucial to foster creativity as well as teaching the technical aspects of wood carving. Encourage participants to use their projects to express themselves, even if they are novices. To spark their imagination, give them ideas and illustrations.

8. Provide Feedback:

Provide constructive criticism as the workshop goes along to aid participants in honing their abilities. This may be an effective tool for developing confidence and growth.

9. Share Resources:

Give participants a list of resources at the conclusion of your workshop, including suggestions for books, websites, and neighborhood woodworking groups where they can continue their woodworking journey.

Offering your own wood carving workshop is a great way to spread knowledge and encourage a passion for this age-old art. It's a fulfilling experience that enables you to meet people who value the same things you do and adds to the development of the woodworking community.

Two exceptional ways to advance your wood carving abilities are to go on woodworking adventures with friends and to run your own wood carving workshop. While working with others promotes a sense of community and challenges your creative abilities, leading a workshop enables you to give back and motivate other woodworkers.

So keep in mind that woodworking is not just about the finished product; it's also about the shared experiences and the thrill of transforming a plain block of wood into a work of art, whether you're carving alongside friends or instructing aspiring woodworkers in a workshop.

Chapter 6:
Reflecting and Showcasing

Hello again, you talented young carvers of wood! In this chapter, we will discuss the final stage of your journey in wood carving, which is also the stage that will provide you with the greatest sense of satisfaction. It is time to give your hard work the spotlight it deserves, share your creations with the world, and take a moment to reflect on how far you've come on this incredible carving journey. It is time to give your hard work the spotlight it deserves.

Displaying Your Carving Masterpieces

Your wood carvings are more than just projects; they are the tangible manifestation of your creativity and the effort you've put in. It is time to provide them with the acknowledgement they have earned. Not only does displaying your carved masterpieces allow you to show off your skills, but it also lends an air of sophistication to the room in which they are displayed. This is how you can go about doing it:

1. Create a Gallery Wall:

Creating a gallery wall to exhibit your wood carvings is rapidly becoming one of the most popular ways to do so. Find a wall that gets a lot of attention in your house and display your carvings in an artistic way there. Create an arrangement that is visually appealing by combining items of varying sizes, styles, and topics. Not only will this give your living space more personality, but it will also give guests something to talk about when they come to visit.

2. Display Shelves:

Adding display shelves is yet another excellent choice that can be made. It is possible to customize these shelves so that they are able to display your wood carvings. You can display your carvings on the shelves by arranging them in a way that highlights their individual characteristics. Display shelves are a smart and convenient way to store and organize your carvings in a way that allows for easy swapping.

3. Rotating Stands:

If you have a collection of smaller carvings, rotating stands might be a good option for displaying them. You are able to display multiple carvings in a condensed area with the help of these stands, which can be placed on tabletops or countertops. You can change their positions on a regular basis to maintain the modern look and feel of your living space.

4. Shadow Boxes:

Displaying intricate or small carvings can be made much easier with the assistance of shadow boxes. These boxes, which have a glass front, are perfect for storing your carvings because they will keep them safe from dust and damage. Displaying your masterpieces in a way that is both distinctive and secure can be accomplished with the help of shadow boxes.

5. Carved Furniture:

Consider incorporating your wood carvings into various pieces of furniture for an approach that is truly one-of-a-kind. This may take the form of a decorative headboard, a chair back with carved details, or even a coffee table with a carved top. These pieces of functional art not only showcase your abilities, but they also fulfill a functional need in the world.

6. Curated Nooks:

You are able to create a curated nook in your home if you have a particular motif or style that you enjoy carving. This can be done in a variety of ways. This could be a section of the room that features wood carvings, other accompanying decorations, and lighting that is designed to highlight your work.

Let's move on to the next step, which is showing off your work with pride, now that you have some suggestions for how to exhibit the masterpieces you've carved out of wood.

Sharing Your Work with Pride

Carving wood is an art form, and art is something that should be experienced by many people and appreciated by all. Do not be bashful about showing off your creations and taking pride in them. It is possible that showing your work to other people will provide you with a satisfying experience. You can approach it in the following ways:

1. Social Media:

In this day and age, social media should be your number one priority. Take photographs of your wood carvings that are of a high quality and upload them to social media sites such as Instagram, Facebook, or Pinterest. Make use of the appropriate hashtags, and participate in online conversations within the woodworking community. You are going to be astounded by the comments and words of encouragement you get.

2. Create a Blog or Website:

If you want to take your wood carving to the next level, you should think about starting a blog or a website that is dedicated to your journey. Tell the tales that lie behind your creations, demonstrate your carving techniques, and discuss the sources of inspiration that guide your work. It is a wonderful opportunity to make connections with other people who share similar interests and to record your development as a woodcarver.

3. Local Art and Craft Fairs:

It is a wonderful way to showcase your wood carvings in a physical setting, and one of the best ways to do so is to take part in local art and craft fairs. You will have the opportunity to engage in conversation with prospective customers, obtain insightful feedback, and form connections with other artists and artisans.

4. Gift Your Creations:

Don't underestimate the joy of gifting your wood carvings to friends and family. It's a thoughtful gesture that not only spreads happiness but also allows you to share your passion with your loved ones.

5. Attend Woodworking Workshops:

Participating in woodworking workshops or classes is an excellent way to network with other woodcarvers and display your creations in a public setting. You can also engage in the sharing of helpful hints and techniques with other enthusiasts, as well as receive insightful commentary.

Now that you've shown everyone in the world what you've been working on, it's time to take things one step further and organize a carving exhibition.

Setting Up a Carving Exhibition

Putting on an exhibition of wood carvings is already an exciting adventure in and of itself. You will have the opportunity to educate people about the world of wood carving, show off your skills, and maybe even make a sale of some of your most impressive works. You can get started by doing the following:

1. Choose a Venue:

Find a location that is appropriate for your exhibition. It could be a community center, an art gallery in the area, or any other location with sufficient space to display your carvings. Check to see that it has sufficient lighting and display space.

2. Curate Your Collection:

Choose the carved wood pieces that you would like to display. Aim for a varied collection that demonstrates both your progression and the range of your abilities as a carver. Create a layout that is aesthetically pleasing with them.

3. Create Information Cards:

Create information cards for each carving, noting the type of wood used, the techniques that were utilized, and the source of inspiration for the piece. This gives the presentation a more personal feel and engages the audience.

4. Promotion and Opening Reception:

Flyers, local newspapers, and social media can all be used to spread the word about your exhibition. Think about holding an opening reception and inviting art lovers from the community, as well as friends and family, to come and admire your work.

5. Sales and Networking:

If you are considering selling your carvings, you should organize your prices in a straightforward manner before you do so. Make the most of this chance to build relationships with prospective customers and fellow artists. It's even possible that people will ask you to do commission work or invite you to future exhibitions.

It's time to examine how far you've come as a woodcarver now that you've had the opportunity to exhibit your work and talk about your interest in the craft.

Reflecting on Your Growth as a Carver

The process of creativity always involves a significant amount of introspection. Consider for a second how far you've come in your career as a wood carver. A journey of self-improvement and self-discovery, reflecting on one's own development is an exciting activity. You can accomplish it in the following ways:

1. Review Your Early Work:

Compare the wood carvings you've done recently to the ones you did when you were first starting out. Take note of the development you've shown in terms of your approach, your creativity, and your attention to detail. Recognize the progress that you've made in the areas that need improvement.

2. Recognize Challenges Overcome:

Consider the difficulties you encountered along the way of your journey in wood carving. Consider how you overcame those challenges and the lessons you gained from the experiences you went through. Your development as a carver can be attributed, in part, to these challenges.

3. Set New Goals:

After you've taken some time to evaluate your progress thus far, it's time to formulate some fresh objectives for your wood carving work. Which skills do you want to advance to the next level in? Which topics or artistic styles do you want to investigate? You can keep your adventure in wood carving exciting and dynamic by setting goals for yourself.

4. Share Your Knowledge:

Share with others the wisdom and experience you've gained throughout your life. You might want to think about leading a class for novices to learn wood carving so that you can share your passion and skills with new enthusiasts. Your development as a carver will benefit greatly from your willingness to teach others what you've discovered.

5. Keep an Art Journal:

Keep a sketchbook, a notebook, or an art journal where you can record your thoughts, ideas, and sketches. Create a record of how you approach your work and how your abilities have developed over time. This journal has the potential to be a source of motivation and an instrument for introspection.

Keep in mind that your adventure in wood carving is a never-ending journey as you come to the end of this chapter. It offers numerous chances for personal development, education, and collaboration. You are not only enriching your own life but also making a contribution to the world of wood carving when you show off your carvings, share your accomplishments with others, organize an exhibition of your work, and think back on how far you've come as a carver. Keep the spirit of adventure alive, and may your journey toward carving bring you nothing but happiness and creative satisfaction.

Conclusion

Within these pages of "Wood Carving for Children," we have embarked on an imaginative adventure, exploring the intricate world of wood carving. You've entered a world of imagination, precision, and craftsmanship from the very first time you picked up your carving tools all the way up until the point where you're reading these final words. Now that we are getting close to the end of this book, it is time to celebrate your journey, think back on the accomplishments you have made, and look forward to the countless opportunities that await you in the world of Cricut crafting and wood carving.

Celebrating Your Wood Carving Journey

The completion of any endeavor is cause for celebration, and the journey you've taken in wood carving is no exception to this rule. It is a testament to your patience, dedication, and creative spirit that you are able to take a simple block of wood and transform it into a work of art. It is essential to take a moment to reflect on how far one has progressed since beginning a task or endeavor. Be proud of your early efforts, even if they resulted in a few nicks and carvings that weren't quite as perfect as you'd like them to be. These experiences served as stepping stones for you, and each one brought you one step closer to becoming the skilled wood carver that you are today.

There are a lot of different ways to celebrate. You might want to consider holding a modest exhibition of some of your favorite creations and inviting members of your family and circle of friends to come and admire your handiwork. When you let other people in on your happiness, they will catch your infectious sense of pride in your work. Displaying your work not only acknowledges your accomplishments but also provides others who are eager to begin their own carving journeys with a source of motivation from which to draw inspiration.

Reflecting on Achievements and Progress

It is imperative that we pause for some self-reflection as we near the end of this excursion. Take some time to think about the things you've accomplished and how far you've come. Compare the self-assurance you had back then, when you first used your carving knife, to the self-assurance you have now. Think back to the first time you used your carving knife. You have gained the ability to read the grain of the wood, carve intricate designs, and infuse life into your creations through your work.

This reflection is not simply an opportunity to admire the tangible products that you have created. Recognizing your own personal development and the skills you've picked up along the way is another important aspect of this process. Your capacity for patience, careful attention to detail, and creative problem-solving is not unique to the realm of wood carving; rather, it is a life skill that will serve you well in any endeavor you undertake.

Keep in mind that maturation is a never-ending process. Regardless of how skilled you become, there is always more that can be learned and improved upon. Embrace the notion that each new project presents an opportunity to improve oneself and grow as a person. Consider your accomplishments, but don't close your eyes to the countless opportunities that lie in store for you in the future.

Looking Forward to Future Projects

It is impossible not to feel a sense of excitement about the future when you think about all that you have accomplished in the past. This book served as both your foundation and your starting point, and now that you've finished it, you're ready to move on to the next step of your journey. Crafting with a Cricut and wood carving are ever-evolving fields that offer new methods, tools, and fashions for you to investigate and experiment with.

The road that lies in front of you is ripe with untapped potential. Think about what kinds of topics or subjects you'd like to delve deeper into in future projects of yours. Do you have an interest in learning more about the art of wood burning or refining your skills in intricate relief carvings? The world of wood carving is as vast as your imagination, and the only thing that will limit your future projects is the level of creativity you bring to them.

However, keep in mind that it is not just about the end result; it is also about the journey that you take to get there. The pleasure of carving lies in the act itself, in the experience of watching a concept materialize through one's own efforts. Therefore, as you look forward to future projects, make sure that you enjoy each step of the process, from choosing the right piece of wood to the last few strokes that you make with your carving tool.

A Note to Parents and Mentors

Your support and advice has been invaluable to the young carvers as they've made their way through this process, and your role in their success cannot be overstated. You have been there to observe their development, to celebrate their successes and commiserate with them over their setbacks, and to foster an atmosphere that has fostered their creative potential. As you've seen, wood carving can teach you valuable lessons about life such as patience, paying attention to detail, and finding solutions to problems. It has instilled a love for craftsmanship and stoked a passion for working with one's hands in those who have experienced it.

Do not stop praising and supporting these up-and-coming young carvers. Participate in their enthusiasm for new projects and, more importantly, make yourself available to lend assistance to them whenever they run into challenges. Through your instruction, they will not only learn how to carve, but they will also develop a passion for woodworking that will remain with them for the rest of their lives. By doing so, you are helping to raise up the next generation of highly skilled artists and woodworkers.

Restating the Message of the Book

Our message has been consistent throughout "Wood Carving for Children," and it is as follows: wood carving is an art form that is both satisfying and enriching, and it is open to participation from people of any age or level of skill. We have made it a priority to remove some of the mystique surrounding the craft by simplifying otherwise difficult methods. We have provided you with the knowledge, tools, and inspiration you need to get started on your journey of wood carving.

This book has encouraged you to embrace the joy of carving, to take pride in your creations, and to find solace and satisfaction in the process of carving rather than simply teaching the technical aspects of carving. Carving beautiful things out of wood isn't just about making pretty things; it's also about personal development, self-expression, and the satisfaction of working with your hands.

Summarizing the Most Important Topics

In order to prepare you for your journey into the world of wood carving, we have covered a variety of topics in this book. We started off with the fundamentals, walking you through the necessary equipment and precautions for safety. The art of carving in the round was investigated, and you were given the tools to bring three-dimensional figures to life. The technique of relief carving was simplified, which made it possible to make intricate patterns on plane surfaces. Your creations were given their finishing touches through the use of finishing techniques and the art of wood burning.

In addition, we delved into the creative side of things by having a conversation about the design process and the significance of drawing motivation from the environment around you. We emphasized how important it is to recognize the pattern of the wood grain and choose the appropriate species of wood for your various projects. It was discussed how to get past typical obstacles so that you would not become disheartened when things got difficult.

Delivering on Our Promise

We have made it our mission to demystify the complex world of wood carving so that even young children can participate in an activity that is accessible, fun, and risk-free. We have made an effort to provide clear and step-by-step instructions that are easy to follow, beginning with your initial introduction to the tools and continuing through your exploration of the various carving techniques. The projects included in this book have been selected with great care to help you build your skills in a step-by-step manner, and the tips and suggestions that are provided are intended to make the experience of carving more enjoyable and rewarding.

Our objective has been to equip you with the skills necessary to become an accomplished wood carver who is able to conceive of and execute their very own one-of-a-kind projects. We have kept our end of the bargain, and as a result, you now have the information and the capabilities necessary to take your wood carving to entirely new levels.

The Key Takeaway

If there's one thing I want you to take away from "Wood Carving for Children," it's the realization that skill is not dependent on one's chronological age. Carving into wood is an ageless art form that can be appreciated by people of all ages. It is a medium that encourages creativity, patience, and an appreciation for the natural wonders of the world around us.

Keep in mind, as you move forward on your journey of wood carving, that the path that lies ahead is filled with an infinite number of possibilities. Your development as a wood carver will be characterized not only by the pieces you produce, but also by the insights you gain and the pleasure you derive from each stroke of your carving tool. Embrace this journey, revel in your accomplishments, and look forward with excitement to what the future holds for you.

The lessons of wood carving are applicable to everyone, regardless of whether you are a young carver learning this art for the first time or a parent or mentor guiding a child's journey through life. They are a constant reminder of the importance of perseverance, patience, and dedication, as well as the joy that comes from the process of creation.

Carving wood is not merely an art form; rather, it is a way of life, a journey that takes us to the center of creativity and craftsmanship.

Now that we have reached the end of this book, I want to encourage you to take out your carving tools, choose a piece of wood, and get started on your next carving project. Allow your imagination to run wild, whether you choose to create a straightforward figure, an intricate relief design, or something completely original. Carry on with your quests of discovery, education, and creation. Your journey into wood carving has only just begun, and the possibilities are as boundless as your imagination. Honor your journey, take stock of all that you've accomplished, and look forward to the future with excitement.

Bonus:
The Essential Tool Maintenance Guide

Your tools are your dependable allies in the world of craftsmanship, whether you're an experienced professional or a budding DIY enthusiast. They have supported you through good times and bad, helping you construct, repair, and produce. But just like any partnership, you need to give your tools some tender loving care to keep them in excellent shape and ready to help you with your next project.

Welcome to the Bonus Chapter of "The Essential Tool Maintenance Guide," our journey through the world of tools and their maintenance. We'll get into the specifics of how to maintain your tools in top condition in this chapter. By the end, you'll have a renewed appreciation for the dependable allies by your side, from your faithful power drill to your dependable hammer.

Why Tool Maintenance Matters

Think of a musician playing on a broken instrument or a chef with a set of dull knives. Their trade's equipment isn't operating at its peak efficiency, which has an impact on the caliber of their work. The same rule is applicable to hobbyists and craftspeople. The performance of tools is compromised when maintenance is neglected, which also shortens their lifespan. A well-maintained tool guarantees more efficient operations, increased safety, and satisfying outcomes.

In order to improve your craft, your finances, and your safety, you should maintain your tools. It's a show of respect for the tools that enable you to make your ideas a reality. Let's dive in and examine the methods and tools required to protect these priceless assets.

Types of Tools and Maintenance

There are many different types of tools, each with a different set of maintenance needs. This chapter will discuss a variety of tools and give you helpful maintenance advice for each. An example of what to expect is as follows:

1. Hand Tools
2. Power Tools
3. Cutting Tools
4. Measuring Tools
5. Specialty Tools
6. Hand Tools

Many professions and do-it-yourself projects rely heavily on hand tools. Your toolbox's workhorses, they can withstand years of abuse. Their lifespan and effectiveness can be maintained with proper maintenance.

A. Wrenches and Pliers

Although the shapes and sizes of these gripping and turning tools vary, their maintenance is generally the same. To prevent rust, keep them clean and dry. For additional protection, wipe them down with a light oil-coated cloth. Examine the teeth and jaws for wear and replace as necessary.

B. Screwdrivers

To drive screws and tighten or loosen various fasteners, screwdrivers are necessary. Avoid using them for tasks that could cause them to slip or strip in order to preserve their tips. They should also be kept clean. Purchasing a high-quality set of replacement bits is a smart move if a tip starts to wear out or become damaged.

C. Hammers

These adaptable tools, which range from ball-peen hammers to framing hammers, need some extra care. Check the head and handle frequently for damage or loose parts because a loose head can be dangerous. Consult the manufacturer's instructions for repair or replacement if you discover any problems.

D. Hand Saws

Hand saws are made to make clean, precise cuts through metal or wood. After using them, clean them to get rid of any pitch or resin, and store them somewhere dry to keep them sharp. When they become dull, think about purchasing a saw sharpening tool or service.

E. Chisels

A chisel works well for shaping and carving wood. By honing the edges with a sharpening stone, you can keep them incredibly sharp. Verify that the handles are stable, and lubricate them occasionally with mineral oil to prevent cracking.

2. Power Tools

The modern-day super heroes of DIY and construction are power tools. They expand your potential but also need extra maintenance to keep them reliable.

A. Drills and Drivers

These adaptable tools, whether corded or cordless, require regular upkeep. The motor vents should be kept clear of debris and the chuck should be cleaned frequently. Don't overwork the motor, and make sure your batteries are charged and stored correctly.

B. Circular Saws

Lumber can be quickly cut with circular saws, but for best results, they must be regularly maintained. Keep the blade well-oiled and sharp. Look for any potentially compromised safety features such as loose bolts, and fix them right away.

C. Grinders

Although powerful, bench grinders and angle grinders can be dangerous if not properly maintained. Verify the safety features of the tool and the grinding discs. Replace worn-out discs and clean the grinder's vents on a regular basis.

D. Sanders

Maintaining your sanding equipment, whether it's a belt sander, orbital sander, or palm sander, is essential for obtaining smooth finishes. If the sandpaper gets worn out, replace it or keep it clean. Inspect the dust collection system and base of the sander for any problems that might impair its performance.

E. Jigsaws

Jigsaws are excellent for making intricate cuts, but they require regular blade replacement and upkeep. Clean the vents and motor of sawdust, and lubricate the blade holder. For precise cuts, keep the baseplate in good condition.

3. Cutting Tools

Cutting tools depend on accuracy and sharpness to function. Maintaining these tools in top shape is essential whether you're cutting through tough materials or creating delicate wooden inlays.

A. Utility Knives

Sharp blades are necessary for safety and effectiveness in all cutting tools, from box cutters to retractable utility knives. When the blade becomes dull or chipped, replace it. You should also occasionally lubricate and clean the moving parts.

B. Chopping and Cutting Boards

Cutting boards are essential in the food preparation process even though they are not traditional tools. Avoid using abrasive scouring pads on them, wash them right away after use, and treat them from time to time with food-grade mineral oil to prevent drying and cracking to maintain their hygiene and longevity.

C. Shears and Scissors

Sharp scissors are your best friend whether you're a seamstress or a crafter. Sharpen the blades frequently, or think about using a professional sharpening service. If necessary, lubricate the pivot point and remove any adhesive residue.

4. **Measuring Tools**

Any project needs precise measurements as a base. Using measuring devices improperly can result in expensive errors and frustration.

A. Tape Measures

The accuracy of tape measures is susceptible to dirt and dust. Check the locking mechanism and clean the tape on a regular basis. It needs to be replaced if it doesn't hold as firmly as it should.

B. Calipers

Calipers are used for precise measurements and come in both digital and analog varieties. Maintain them by lubricating them and changing the batteries in digital calipers as necessary. Analog calipers should have their accuracy periodically checked against a reference standard.

C. Levels

For ensuring level and straight surfaces, levels are necessary. Protect the bubble vials from damage by keeping them in a cushioned case. Verify if there is any misalignment, and if so, have them calibrated.

5. **Specialty Tools**

Specialty tools are designed for particular jobs, such as plumbing tools and woodworking jigs. Regardless of how they are maintained, diligence is essential to keeping them in good working order.

A. Pipe Wrenches

Pipe wrenches are essential for plumbing professionals and do-it-yourself projects. Check the jaws for wear on a regular basis, and replace them if necessary. To ensure smooth operation, lubricate the moving parts and clean the threads.

B. Woodworking Jigs

Jigs for woodworking improve your projects' accuracy and consistency. Maintain their cleanliness and check that all of their parts, including the stops and guides, are firmly fastened. To ensure accuracy, periodically check their alignment.

C. Welding Equipment

Tools and equipment used for welding have specific maintenance requirements. Maintain clean, spatter-free welding tips, check for leaks in gas hoses and regulators, and regularly replace worn consumables.

You've learned the value of taking good care of your tools and how to maintain them effectively as we've traveled through "The Essential Tool Maintenance Guide." Your tools are more than just inert things; they are your collaborators in creation and your dream-enablers. Your work will become more effective, safe, and ultimately more satisfying if you put time and effort into keeping them maintained.

Remember that maintaining your tools will improve the quality of your work and ensure that you can count on them for many years to come in addition to helping them last longer. So, before starting your next project, stop to appreciate the tools you have in your possession and realize that, because of the attention you've given them, you are equipped to handle any difficulties that may arise.

With this information at your disposal, you are well on your way to mastering tool maintenance. So create away, and may your tools always be dependable and effective for you.

Video Tutorials

YouTube has become a veritable knowledge vault in the digital age, offering countless tutorials on a wide range of topics. The tutorial "Wood Carving for Beginners" is one of these that has received a lot of attention. This video promises to walk you through the necessary steps whether you're a beginner or an experienced woodworker looking to explore the world of carving.

1. Tools and Materials: The first part of the video introduces the materials and tools needed for wood carving. To ensure a secure and successful carving experience, it's crucial to have the appropriate tools on hand, including chisels and gouges as well as safety gear like gloves and eye protection.

2. Selecting Your Wood: The choice of wood is an important aspect of wood carving, and the video goes into detail about the kinds of wood that are best for beginners. It draws attention to the differences between softwood and hardwood and enables viewers to make an informed decision.

3. Basic Carving Techniques: When you're prepared and have your wood ready, the video immediately starts shooting. It illustrates basic carving techniques like working with the grain, utilizing the push and pull techniques, and using the right hand position.

4. Safety Measures: The tutorial emphasizes safety at all times and offers vital advice on keeping your tools under control, keeping them sharp, and working in a well-ventilated area. This video clearly illustrates the importance of safety.

5. Step-by-Step Projects: The tutorial presents step-by-step projects, starting with straightforward designs and progressively moving up to more complex ones, to make the learning process more interesting. This methodical approach enables beginners to develop their abilities and self-assurance.

6. Finishing and Sanding: The process doesn't end with the carving. Sanding and other finishing touches are also covered in the video. It explains how to polish finished wood carvings, sand down rough edges, and add finishing touches.

7. Sealing and Staining: An appropriate finish is necessary for a polished wood carving. To improve the appearance and tensile strength of your creations, this section of the tutorial discusses sealing methods and staining choices.

8. Troubleshooting and Tips: The tutorial doesn't leave you hanging because difficulties can arise for any beginner. It addresses typical problems like splintering and provides practical advice to get past these obstacles.

9. Project Ideas: The video also offers imaginative project suggestions, encouraging beginners to practice their newly acquired wood carving abilities. There are countless options, whether you're looking for a personalized gift, a useful item, or a decorative ornament.

10. Community and Resources: The tutorial urges viewers to get involved in the offline and online woodworking scene to meet other enthusiasts and learn more. For those looking to increase their knowledge, it also recommends books, discussion boards, and other resources.

Anyone looking to start a wood carving journey should check out "Wood Carving for Beginners." This YouTube video is a great place for those just learning the craft of wood carving to start because of its clear and succinct presentation, educational tips, and interesting project ideas. Remember that practice makes perfect, so don't let minor failures deter you from continuing to carve. Stay safe and enjoy the process as you turn a piece of ordinary wood into a work of art.

Printed in Great Britain
by Amazon